9 PALINDROMES PARAPR

POSTERS

Fun for People
Who Almost Qualify
For Mensa

Rand Gee

For reproduction permission, send request to
Rand Gee
PO Box 513   Pentwater, Michigan 49449-0513

First Edition, May, 2017

Published by: Rand Gee
Illustrated by: Ken Kuzia
Distributed by: Lulu.com

Library of Congress Cataloging-in-Publication Data is Available

ISBN 978-1-365-84125-5

ISBN 978-1-365-84125-5
90000

9 781365 841255

Printed in the United States of America.

CONTENTS

ACKNOWLEDGEMENTS

FAMILY & FRIENDS

Thanks to my wife, Nancy who shares funny items with me. My son, Matt, who has a quick wit and sense of humor keeps me looking for stories, and laughing at myself. Ken, my business partner, provides another funny take on life and keeps me thinking. My college buddies Bill S, Bill V, Roger A, and Tom B, who are much smarter than I am, took the time to teach me things I would have never learned at college. And, of course, Fred and Richard who looked on and laughed as they watched a myriad of people look at my posters, wag their heads "No", and say, "What?"

GRAPHIC ARTIST

Ken Kuzia is an artist who paints, sketches, and photographs interesting people and places. He particularly enjoys and excels at digitally enhancing photographs to produce eye-catching art. The cover image he photographed and enhanced. Read more about Ken at the end of the book. Visit his website at:

http://vicartgroup.wixsite.com/the-art-of-ken-kuzia

DISCLAIMER

Any names, characters, businesses, places, events, and incidents are the products of the author's imagination and used in a fictitious manner. Any resemblance to actual events or actual persons, living or dead, is purely coincidental and unintentional. The possibility exists that some Mensa members will be offended by the lack of challenge my content presents, but that's a risk I am willing to take.

SPECIAL THANKS

Thanks for your input and editing!

Roger Au

Mark Benner

Tom Bylsma

Matt Gee

Buz Graettinger

Ken Kuzia

Fred McHugh

Bill Schmidt

Richard St. Denis

Bill Van Horne

FORWARD

I live with Mensa people*: a son, his friends, a few relatives, a myriad of neighbors, and a hand-full of village residents.

> *Mensa is the largest and oldest, high IQ society in the world, and is open to people who score at the 98th percentile or higher on a standardized, supervised IQ, or other approved intelligence test.
>
> Mensa International and Mensa.org

But, let me be clear. I'm not a Mensa member. I'm close! I can answer the test questions correctly, but not within the required thirty minutes. Am I jealous? Yeah, I think so. On the other hand, while I'm not a genius, maybe I possess a better-developed, though dark and wry, sense of humor. And, perhaps I enjoy interaction more, so I like sharing my humor and stimulating laughter! Hence, this book.

Palindromes make me think! I am in awe of the bright people who can construct such complicated letter sequences. One of my college mates, Bill, had to educate me on Mensa and Palindromes and the rules that define them. So, I have been enamored and quietly in awe of palindromes and their creators since about 1967.

Paraprosdokians, on the other hand, make me laugh. I love the irony and the twists that they bring. I enjoy their swift and unexpected changes of direction or intent. But, I would have missed them all if Bill, the Mensa member, hadn't educated me on them as well.

Some bulletin board posters provide a natural and visual extension of paraprosdokians by providing twisted or ironic entertainment. Those that do, catch my attention. I love it when they give me a quiet belly laugh, and a concept sticks with me for the day, bringing a smile with each reflection.

The downside to enjoying palindromes, paraprosdokians, and wry, twisted posters is that I have a very limited scope of people with whom I can share my discoveries. Delivery to the dull person elicits a response of confusion, and I have to explain what I'm laughing about. With Mensa members, I usually get an entirely different reaction: "Yeah. So?" And, with others in the middle of the intelligence spectrum, I likely prove myself a Dolt, Dork, Freak, Geek, Nerd, or Weirdo! They screw up their faces and look at me like I am strange – and, I laugh even more.

Hope you think deeply and laugh heartily as you read!

THE POSTER EXPERIMENT

Why a collection of posters? I live in a small, safe, conservative, village in rural Michigan. In my opinion, if you are the thinking sort, then this village is, too often, mind-numbingly dull! Wanting to keep my brain active and to stave off natural, age-related, cognitive decline, I continue to create activities and experiments that challenge my thinking. Out of this effort was born the "Poster Experiment".

The local post office is the cultural hub of the village. During the flood of summer residents, vacationers, and tourists, the post office is where the locals go to escape the hubbub, retrieve their mail, and learn of village news. During the winter months, when only about 200 residents choose to endure the cold, snow, and depressing, grey-dome sky, the post office is one of three places open during the day. Villagers go to the post office to retrieve their mail and to ensure that they aren't the only ones still alive in the village.

There are two side-by-side post office bulletin boards that have become a central communication point for villagers. The bulletin boards are like all the others you have seen with at least 10,000 punctures and a plethora of push pins, but always one fewer than needed when you're hanging a posting. The two boards overflow in the summer with ads for boats, fishing gear, fishing charters, campers, rental property, entertainment, church services, and self-help groups, all slightly overlapping each other. From November through May, the content wanes and board space opens because there isn't enough happening in the village to warrant announcements.

Technically the bulletin boards are the property of the U.S. Post Office, but the Post Master here has learned over the years that strict policing isn't required. Three residents have appointed themselves Bulletin Board Czars. They choose to police the bulletin boards, ensuring that no inappropriate materials are posted. They want the content of the boards to reflect the conservative, polite, gracious, sharing, caring community that we are (at least on the surface).

Take my word for it! The czars are fastidious and relentless! They groom and arranging the boards daily to ensure maximum exposure for all posted information. Overlapping posters aren't tolerated! Outdated posters are ripped from the boards - with forceful purpose - as soon as they expire. Political posters don't last! Ads for major businesses are never allowed! A poster with the slightest hint of comment about another resident is strictly forbidden and may even elicit a scolding conversation. The Czars see their role as protecting civic integrity!

After observing the results of czars' actions, I decided that they prune the boards with an OCD nature. The more I thought about their persnickety monitoring, the more I became powerless to a challenge. I had to test how long a humorous, or sarcastic, or somewhat moronic poster would remain on the board.

After a few days of pondering my experiment, I began creating posters using ironic ideas and concepts that made me think or laugh. With purpose the posters contained no libelous, lascivious, lewd, politically-biased, or scandalous materials. They just presented an opportunity for a thinking person to read something that would produce a smile. For people who didn't want to think or be bothered, the posters would produce, at most, a shake of the head and no further thought.

I chose summer as the best time to test. The czars' behavior suggests that they winter elsewhere and only do their civic duty April through September. Most of the posters contained in this book were tested on the bulletin boards during July and August to give post office patrons maximum opportunity to enjoy my humor.

Of course testing meant that I had to visit the post office about the same time each day to monitor how long my poster remained on display. As soon as one poster was removed, I mounted a new test poster in a different place on the bulletin board and always in a way that didn't cover other, legitimate postings.

The hypothesis being tested states was that the czars would not experience the humor in the posters, deem them unworthy of bulletin board space, and immediately remove them to protect the village from inappropriate representation of our culture and values. I suspected that the czars would rip my posters from their positions, shred them, and toss them into the recycle bin.

Now, I never observed the czars in action, nor did I ever talk with them about their poster removal decision-making. In fact, I don't have any personal evidence that the Czars actually exist, or that they ever removed my posters. However, someone regularly removed my postings, and it's more entertaining to think that the czars are the culprits. The Post Master commented once that he observed the backs of the czars as they did their policing work. He could see their backs through the post boxes as he was throwing mail. He says the czars are real, and they do police the boards daily. But, like Sasquatch, I've never seen one.

One real outcome of the experiment confirmed that there must be an unspoken set of posting criteria, and the majority of my posters must have fallen outside proper limits! Most posters remained less than a day. Three lasted two days. One, an ad for lost dentures, lasted 4 days, until I scratched out "Lost", wrote "Found", and added the note of, "Thanks! Now I can eat steak again." Meantime, other posters for a kayak, an older SUV, and an ad for a lost cat remained and must have legitimately met the Czars' requirements.

Before beginning the experiment, I took the Post Master into my confidence. I alerted him whenever new posters were hung. He's a guy that thinks keenly and likes a deep belly laugh! He seemed anxious to see what would happen as I posted my test pages. To some extent, I think he wanted to be an active part of the test. But, as Post Master and official guardian of the bulletin boards, he wasn't permitted to join my team. He offered quiet support and, in his heart-of hearts, he was a member, in absentia.

I muse about the czars conducting a short Papal-like conclave in the post office lobby to express their frustration and to remove yet another of my "inappropriate" posters. I don't believe the Czars ever determined who was "trespassing" on their boards. In my mind's eye, now that I am writing about this, I am struck by the idea that, perhaps, there are community members that act as agents for the Czars by passing along intel regarding new postings. Hummmm. Undercover agents of sorts?

The experiment clearly demonstrated that there are keen thinkers in the village who enjoy a challenging thought or bit of humorous sarcasm. The Post Master and I independently witnessed a few people chuckling or pointing out a poster to another patron. My experiment did produce intended smiles.

A bothersome outcome was demonstrated by people who missed the humor and thought the posters were actually authentic. For example, comments were made about the dentures and how awful it must be to lose your teeth. The Free Chickens poster produced authentic anger and frustration for a chap who wanted the chickens. He approached the Post Master with a serious complaint saying that he'd read the poster five times, and still couldn't find a phone number. He was seriously perturbed and totally missed the humor about the chicken coops versus chicken sedans. And, he missed taking his free chicken printed on each tab.

Overall, the results of the experiment were no harm - no foul. Thanks to the czars' reverent and unceasing civic duty, no one went into shock, no one suffered a serious medical emergency, and no one had a psychological meltdown. No one was embarrassed, and no one was demeaned. No political pressure was applied. No marching herd of protesters arose. But, I can imagine that the three Czars were distressed.

In my opinion, the experiment was an absolute success because, with every posting, I had a belly laugh! And, I still believe lots of other people smiled, as well!

PALINDROMES

Here's what my friend Bill, the Mensa member, explained to me, before Wikipedia was invented:

> "A palindrome is a word, number, or phrase where the sequence of characters reads the same backward or forward, such as madam or kayak, with allowances made for capital letters, punctuation, and word dividers. A catchy example is: "A man, a plan, a canal, Panama!" "Was it a car or a cat I saw?"
>
> Bill Schmidt, 1967

Wikipedia added:

> The word "palindrome" was coined by Ben Jonson in the 17th century from the Greek roots palin ("again") and dromos ("way, direction")."

> You may need this information if you take the Mensa Entrance Exam: Ben Jonson was a playwright, poet, actor, and literary critic of the 17th century, whose artistry exerted a lasting impact upon English poetry and stage comedy. He popularized the comedy of humours. He is best known for satirical plays and for lyric poetry. He's generally regarded as the second most important English playwright after William Shakespeare.
>
> Definition and information courtesy of Wikipedia.

Here's my collection:

FREE CHICKENS

I have too many chickens and they need good homes. All hens and no roosters to wake you in the morning. Get your chickens and get them housed before the Village Council bans the raising of chickens in the Village.

If you are building a chicken coop, be sure to build in two doors to meet the new fire codes. Also, be aware that if you install four doors the structure will fall under a different code because it will be a chicken sedan and not a coupe.

TAKE ONE	TAKE ONE	TAKE ONE	TAKE ONE	TAKE ONE	TAKE ONE	TAKE ONE

A but tuba.

A car, a man, a maraca.

A dog, a plan, a canal: pagoda.

A dog! A panic in a pagoda!

A lad named E. Mandala.

A man, a plan, a canal: Panama.

A man, a plan, a cat, a ham, a yak, a yam, a hat, a canal-Panama!

A new order began, a more Roman age bred Rowena.

A nut for a jar of tuna.

A Santa at NASA.

A Santa dog lived as a devil God at NASA.

A slut nixes sex in Tulsa.

LOST MY DENTURES

- Took Out at Beach to Swim

- Someone Shook Blanket

- Chompin' at the Bit to Get Them Back!

- Inscribed "Bill" on Top & Bottom Plate

- Tooth Fairy Will Pay Reasonable Finder's Fee!

221-555-1212   221-555-1212   221-555-1212   221-555-1212   221-555-1212   221-555-1212   221-555-1212   221-555-1212   221-555-1212   221-555-1212   221-555-1212   221-555-1212

A tin mug for a jar of gum, Nita.

A Toyota! Race fast, safe car! A Toyota!

A Toyota's a Toyota.

Able was I ere I saw Elba.

Acrobats stab orca.

Aerate pet area.

Ah, Satan sees Natasha!

Aibohphobia (fear of palindromes).

Air an aria.

Al lets Della call Ed Stella.

Amen icy cinema.

Amore, Roma.

Amy, must I jujitsu my ma?

— LOST CAT —

- PROWLS AT NIGHT.
- MEAN AND PROBABLY SCARED.
- LIKELY TO BE HUNGRY.
- WILL BITE IF CORNERED.
- NO COLLAR.
- ANSWERS TO NO NAME.
- LAST SEEN AT CORNER OF 4TH & COLLINS STS.

* IF YOU SEE THIS CAT JUST FEED AND WATER IT. SHE MAY COME HOME SOON!

Animal loots foliated detail of stool lamina.

Anne, I vote more cars race Rome to Vienna.

Are Mac 'n' Oliver ever evil on camera?

Are we not drawn onward to new era?

Are we not drawn onward, we few, drawn onward to new era?

Are we not pure? "No sir!" Panama's moody Noriega brags. "It is garbage!" Irony dooms a man; a prisoner up to new era.

Art, name no tub time. Emit but one mantra.

As I pee, sir, I see Pisa!

Avid diva.

Baby Bab.

Bar an arab.

Barge in! Relate mere war of 1991 for a were-metal Ernie grab!

STICK
FOR SALE

Found 2015
Almost New ◆ Only Used 2-3 Times
Excellent Condition! ◆ Only 4 tooth marks & 3 tiny
scratches.

Unfortunately Marco Polo (pictured above) wasn't
smart enough to get across the bridge for dinner. He
passed 2 months ago and we kept his stick. But, the
stick reminds us too much of Marco and makes us
sad. We desperately need to find a new home for the
stick! We can take cash, check, or major credit card.
$35.00

232-555-1212   232-555-1212   232-555-1212   232-555-1212   232-555-1212   232-555-1212   232-555-1212   232-555-1212   232-555-1212   232-555-1212   232-555-1212   232-555-1212

Bird rib.

Bombard a drab mob.

Borrow or rob?

Bursitis Rub.

Bush saw Sununu swash sub.

Cain: a maniac.

"Cain, a motor erotomaniac was Eve," said I as Eve saw Cain, "a motor erotomaniac!"

Camp Mac.

Campus motto: Bottoms up Mac.

Cigar? Toss it in a can. It is so tragic.

Daedalus: nine. Peninsula: dead.

Dammit, I'm mad!

Decaf and DNA faced.

Have You
Seen This Bird?

This bird has been trained to love French fries. Knows one word of English but always says in threes: "Mine, Mine, Mine" and says it to be grateful when fed. Will you feed this bird?

Take Tab where you will feed.   Thanks!

At KFC | At Taco Bell | At McDonalds | At A&W Root Beer | At Burger King | At Wendy's | At Dairy Queen | At Arby's | At White Castle | At Steak 'n Shake | At Sonic | At Long John Silvers | At Big Boy

Dee saw a seed.

Degas, are we not drawn onward, no? In union, drawn onward to new eras aged?

Delia saw I was ailed.

Denim axes examined.

"Dennis and Edna dine," said I, as Enid and Edna sinned.

Dennis and Edna sinned.

Dennis sinned.

Dennis, Eve saw Eden if as a fine dew, as Eve sinned.

Dennis, Nell, Edna, Leon, Nedra, Anita, Rolf, Nora, Alice, Carol, Leo, Jane, Reed, Dena, Dale, Basil, Rae, Penny, Lana, Dave, Denny, Lena, Ida, Bernadette, Ben, Ray, Lila, Nina, Jo, Ira, Mara, Sara, Mario, Jan, Ina, Lily, Arne, Bette, Dan, Reba, Diane, Lynn, Ed, Eva, Dana, Lynne, Pearl, Isabel, Ada, Ned, Dee, Rena, Joel, Lora, Cecil, Aaron, Flora, Tina, Arden, Noel, and Ellen sinned.

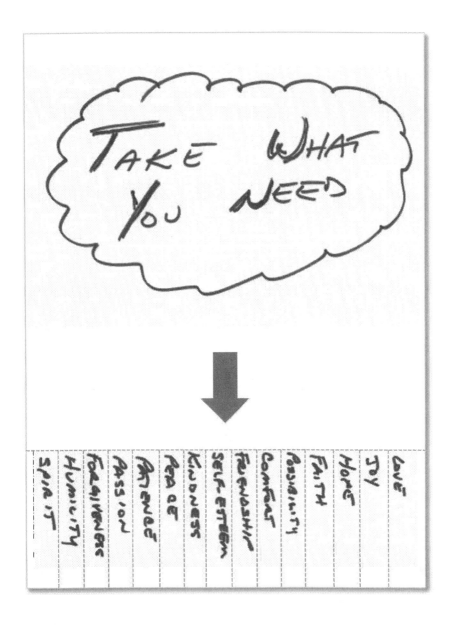

Dentist? Sit Ned.

Depardieu, go razz a rogue I draped.

Desserts I desire not, so long no lost one rise distressed.

Desserts, I stressed!

"Desserts, sis?" (Sensuousness is stressed).

Devil never even lived.

Dial Laid.

Did Hannah see bees? Hannah did.

Did I cite Operas Are Poetic? I did.

Did I do, O God, did I as I said I'd do? Good! I did.

Did I draw Della too tall, Edward? I did?

Did mom pop? Mom did.

Didi won straw warts. Now I did.

Be The First To
Like This Pole!

Don't Miss This Opportunity
<u>For One Day Only,</u>
Show People That You Like This
Pole

(Was taped to a flag pole at the Post Office)

Do geese see God?

Do good? I? No! Evil anon I deliver. I maim nine more hero-men in Saginaw, sanitary sword a-tuck, Carol, I — lo! — rack, cut a drowsy rat in Aswan. I gas nine more hero-men in Miami. Reviled, I (Nona) live on. I do, O God!

Dogma: I am God.

Do nine men interpret? Nine men. I nod.

Do not bob to nod.

Do offer ref food.

Do, O God, no evil deed! Live on! Do good!

Doc, note, I Dissent. A fast never prevents a fatness. I diet on cod.

Dog doo? Good God!

Dog! No poop on God!

Dogma in my hymn: I am God.

Dogma: I am God.

Free to Any Willing Home

My girlfriend does not like my beagle Molly. So I have to re-home her. She is purebred from a wealthy area and I have had her 4 years. She likes to play games. Not totally trained. Has long hair so she's a little high maintenance, especially her nails, but she loves having them done. Stays up all night yapping but sleeps while I work. Only eats the best, most expensive food. Will NEVER greet you at the door after a long day or give you unconditional love when you are down. Does not bite but she can be mean as Hell!

So — anyone interested in my 30 year old, selfish, wicked, gold-digging girlfriend? Come and get her! Me and my dog want her re-homed ASAP!

235-555-1212 235-555-1212 235-555-1212 235-555-1212 235-555-1212 235-555-1212 235-555-1212 235-555-1212 235-555-1212 235-555-1212 235-555-1212 235-555-1212 235-555-1212

Don't nod.

Doom mood.

Dr. Awkward.

Drab as a fool, aloof as a bard.

Drat Saddam! Mad dastard!

Drat such custard!

Draw Kwan awkward.

Draw nine men inward.

Draw O Caesar. Erase a coward.

Draw pupil's lip upward.

Draw Ward.

Draw, O coward!

Drawer's reward.

REWARD!

"EDDIE"

Black, and grey with white markings on neck and chest, rescued male cat. Approximately 6 years old and spayed. Wears red collar with tags (not shown). Slightly overweight. Friendly, affectionate, and vocal – mews all day and night demanding attention. Won't stay off counter tops. Eats directly from unattended plates. Pushes glasses, vases, and bottles off counters and shelves onto floor. Is basically healthy but has a few, various, expensive chronic ailments. Hasn't learned any tricks and doesn't do anything of interest. Overall, great companion.

Will give this cat to whoever returns my car keys lost around 1st and Main Street last Thursday.

237-555-1212 | 237-555-1212 | 237-555-1212 | 237-555-1212 | 237-555-1212 | 237-555-1212 | 237-555-1212 | 237-555-1212 | 237-555-1212 | 237-555-1212 | 237-555-1212 | 237-555-1212

Drawn onward.

Drawn, I sit; serene rest is inward.

Dubya won? No way, bud.

Dumb mud.

Ed, I hung a gnu hide!

Ed, I saw Harpo Marx ram Oprah W. aside.

Egad! A base life defiles a bad age.

Egad! A base tone denotes a bad age.

Egad! An adage!

Egad! Loretta has Adams as mad as a hatter. Old age!

Egad! No bondage?

Elba Kramer saw I was remarkable.

Elite tile.

Elk rap song? No sparkle.

UNICORN RIDING LESSONS

Perfect for your Princess!

Rainbow Sunshine Farms on Pleasant Lane

Lessons Include:
- Fanciful Frolicking in Meadows
- Horn Polishing & Sparkle Adding
- Tail Bradding & Bedazzling

- Birthday Parties Welcome
- Ask About Irish Discounts
- Complimentary Hot Chocolate, Marshmallows, and Smiles

353-555-1212 | 353-555-1212 | 353-555-1212 | 353-555-1212 | 353-555-1212 | 353-555-1212 | 353-555-1212 | 353-555-1212 | 353-555-1212 | 353-555-1212 | 353-555-1212 | 353-555-1212

Em to Greg: Gad! A dagger got me!

Emily's sassy lime.

Emu love volume.

Enid and Edna dine.

Ere I saw Elba, able was I ere.

Ergo, a ogre.

Erupt on Naomi? I moan, "Not pure!"

Eva use Suave.

Eva, can I stab bats in a cave?

Eve damned Eden. Mad Eve!

Eve saw Diamond, erred. No maid was Eve!

"Evil axis", sides reversed, is "six alive".

Evi saves God dogs (evasive).

For A Good Time . . .

Call Prime Time . . .
235-711-1317

235-711-1317 235-711-1317 235-711-1317 235-711-1317 235-711-1317 235-711-1317 235-711-1317 235-711-1317 235-711-1317 235-711-1317 235-711-1317 235-711-1317

Evil did I dwell, lewd I did live.

Evil olive.

Evil rats on no star live.

Evil, a sin, is alive.

Ew! Eat a ewe?

Flee to me, remote elf.

Gabe's on a nosebag.

Gaby H.'s art saved Eva's trashy bag.

Galoots, too, lag.

Gate man sees name, garage man sees name tag.

Gnu dung.

Go deliver a dare, vile dog!

Go dog.

Go hang a salami, I'm a lasagna hog.

Caution: Schools Are Teaching . . .

$$A = \pi r^2$$

But Pie $\cancel{r}^2$

Pie r Round

Cornbread r^2

God lived as a devil dog.

God lives, evil dog.

God saw I was dog.

God, Art! Name no pup "One Mantra Dog."

God! A red nugget! A fat egg under a dog!

God's dog.

Goddamn mad dog!

Goldenrod-adorned log.

Golf? No sir, prefer prison-flog.

Harass Sarah.

Harass sensuousness, Sarah.

Harpo: not on Oprah.

He did, eh?

He nips; send a man Anan! A madness pin eh?

He won snow, eh?

He won! Killer! Rad Darrell I know, eh?

Hey, Roy! Am I mayor? Yeh!

Hon? I see bees in – OH!

I did, did I?

I made border bard's drowsy swords; drab, red robed am I.

I prefer pi.

I roamed under it as a tired, nude Maori.

I saw a crow, orca was I.

I saw desserts; I'd no lemons, alas no melon! Distressed was I.

I saw Ed under Deb's bed; red, nude was I.

I, man, am regal; a German am I.

Question for Today

If you had to choose drinking wine every day or being skinny, which would you choose?

Red? OR **White?**

I'm a lasagna, bang a salami.

I'm a pup, am I?

I'm a tune nut, am I?

I'm a fool; aloof am I.

If I fret, fasten nets after Fifi.

If I had a hi-fi…

In a regal age ran I.

In word salad, alas, drown I.

In words, alas, drown I.

In words, drown I.

Is it I? It is I!

Kay, a red nude, peeped under a yak.

Lag not, Eno! No gong! Get up! Put eggnog on one-ton gal!

Lager, sir, is regal.

THOUGHT FOR TODAY

**STOP TRYING TO
MAKE EVERYONE HAPPY!
YOUR DON'T HAVE
SUPER HERO POWERS
AND . . .**

**YOU ARE NOT
TEQUILA!**

Laid at a dial.

Laminated E.T. animal.

Late metal.

Lay a wallaby baby ball away, Al.

Leon's noel.

Lepers repel.

Let O'Hara gain an inn in a Niagara hotel.

Let Omro open one poor motel.

Liam's mail.

Lid off a daffodil.

Lion oil.

Lisa Bonet ate no basil.

Live dirt up a side track carted is a putrid evil.

Live evil.

Henrietta Needs Help

Went to pet area at Kroger. They were out of my usual brand of turtle food. I would have bought the store brand if Henrietta weren't so picky.

If you have a couple days of Nutrina Zoo Med Brand Turtle Food, **please** leave some in bag below.

I can't pay you now – don't want to leave money in bag – but if you leave your e-mail, I will contact you so I can mail you a check or some delicious snacks.

Henrietta will definitely appreciate your generosity! Thanks in Advance!

Live no evil! Live on evil!

Live not on evil.

Live, O Devil, revel ever! Live! Do evil!

Lived on Decaf; faced no Devil.

Llama mall.

Lonely Tylenol.

Loops at a spool.

Ma has a ham.

Ma is a madam, as I am.

Ma is a nun, as I am.

Ma is as selfless as I am.

"Ma," Jerome raps pot top, "Spare more jam!"

Mad as Adam.

Madam in Eden, I'm Adam.

WISHFUL THINKING

**What Steve Harvey
Always Wants to Say
by End of Family Feud Game!**

Madam, I'm Adam.

Madam, in Eden I'm Adam.

Madame, not one man is selfless; I name not one, madam.

Mail Liam.

Malayalam.

Maps, DNA, and spam.

Marge lets Norah see Sharon's telegram.

Marge, lets send a sadness telegram.

Margot trades used art to gram.

Max exam.

May a moody baby doom a yam?

Meet animals; laminate 'em.

Mega gem.

Mirror rim.

Understanding Women

Finally available in paperback!

To Order:
241-555-5512
$1195.00
While Supplies Last!
Hand Delivered to Your Door!

Mother Eve's noose we soon sever, eh Tom?

Mr. Owl ate my metal worm.

Murder for a jar of red rum.

Must sell at tallest sum.

My gay rub won, Star. Rats now bury a gym.

My gym.

Nail a tired rotini in it, order Italian!

Naive Evian.

Name no one man.

Name no side in Eden, I'm mad! A maid I am, Adam mine; denied is one man.

Name not one man.

Name now one man.

Name tarts? No, medieval slave, I demonstrate man!

Name's Abel, a male, base man.

MISSING

PERIOD KEY
FROM MY KEYBOARD

Key was last seen on my keyboard on my desk on Lowell Street when I was working on a letter I don't know what happened to the key It must have popped off or someone removed it while I was at the Post Office Sometimes when I write I get really angry or frustrated when the words don't flow and then I pound on the keyboard Probably loosened the period key causing it to pop off This is a mental disorder for which I am being treated and for which I take medication Then I missed a dose and life went wacky What can you do We all have issues that we face in life We try to face them but sometime progress is slow I face this issue every day and try to get better day by day It is all about living in the moment I think that one moment I was living in was bad and now my period key is missing Cash reward Leave the key and your name with Post Master and he will put in my box 1287 I'll get back to you with cash and a big Thank You

Naomi, did I moan?

Nat tan.

Nate bit a tibetan.

Ned, I am a maiden.

Ned! go gag Ogden!

Neil, an alien.

Nella risks all: "I will ask Sir Allen!"

Nemo's omen.

Never odd or even.

Niagara, eh? I hear again!

Niagara, O roar again!

No "x" in "Nixon."

No cab, no tuna nut on bacon.

No demerits tire me, Don.

FOUND DOG

CORNER OF 2ND AND VICTORIA STREET

WE'VE BONDED & NOW WE'RE BROS!
I NAMED HIM SMILEY.
SO, HE'S STAYING!

DON'T CALL!   DON'T MAKE IT WEIRD!

No devil lived on.

No evil shahs live on.

No lemon, no melon.

No lemons, no melon.

No sir! Away! A papaya war is on.

No trace, not one carton.

No, I save on final perusal – a sure plan if no evasion.

No, I tan at a nation.

No, I told Ed "lotion."

No, it can assess an action.

No, it is open on one position.

No, it is opposed: art sees trade's opposition.

No, it is opposition.

No, it never propagates if I set a gap or prevention.

MISSING

Last seen on my desk in the garage at 298 Wythe. Initials scratched on top. Gum stuck to top, as well. Drive has been in the family for years. Has sentimental value. Also has a few family pictures, some of questionable content.

REWARD – for returning. No Questions Asked!

BTW - What kind of sick mind takes people's floppy drives? I don't care about the mower, gas can, golf clubs, or wheel barrel in the garage. You can have those! Bring my disks back!

Do the right thing!   Call 245-555-1212

No, it's Abe Sebastion.

No, it's a bar of gold – a bad log for a bastion.

No, Mel Gibson is a casino's big lemon.

No, Miss Lianne draws as Warden nails Simon.

No, sir, away! A papaya war is on!

No, Sir, panic is a basic in a prison.

No, son! Onanism's a gross orgasm sin – a no-no, son!

No, tie it on.

No trace; not one carton.

Nod off, obese boffo don.

Nola's salon.

Norma is as selfless as I am, Ron.

Not a banana baton.

Now do I repay a period won.

T O D A Y

Today was the worst day ever!
And don't try to convince me that
There's something good in every day
Because when you take a closer look,
The world is a pretty evil place
Even if
Some goodness does shines through once in a
while
Satisfaction and Happiness don't last.
And it's not true
It's all in the mind and heart
Because
True Happiness can be obtained
Only if one's surroundings are good
It's not true that good exists
I'm sure you can agree that
The reality
Creates
My Attitude
It's all beyond my control
And you'll never in a million years hear me say
that
Today was a good day
(Now read from the bottom up.)

Now ere we nine were held idle here, we nine were won.

Now I draw an award. I won!

Now I see bees I won.

Now I won.

Now no swim on mon.(Upside down).

Nurse, I spy gypsies. Run!

Nurses run.

Geronimo, no minor ego.

O, stone, be not so.

Oh no! Don Ho!

Oh, cameras are macho.

Olson is in Oslo.

On a clover, if alive, erupts a vast, pure evil; a fire volcano.

LOST . . .

Photo of My Dog

I always carry this photo of my black lab on my clipboard. I paid five dollars to have this photo taken in a dark room of a hotel that I wasn't supposed to be in. I don't want this photo to land in the wrong hands. This photo has real sentimental value to me and finding it is important!

Substantial for Reward!
243-555-1212

I'm . . . Heart Broken !

Oozy rat in a sanitary zoo.

Oprah deified Harpo.

Otto made Ned a motto.

Otto sees Otto.

Pa's a sap.

Party boobytrap.

Pass mom's sap.

Pets tell Abe ballet step.

Pooh animals slam in a hoop.

Pool loop.

Poor Dan is in a droop.

Pot top.

Au Revoir!

Don't try to find me! I have finally escaped my "Master's" wicked clutches!

To others I say, " Rejoins moi"!

Bite the hand that feeds you!

Viva la Liberté!

Pull up if I pull up.

Pull up, Eva, we're here! Wave! Pull up!

Pusillanimity obsesses Boy Tim in All Is Up.

Put Eliot's toilet up.

Race fast, safe car!

Rae hired Leif as a fielder, I hear.

Rail delivers reviled liar.

Rats at a bar grab at a star.

Rats live on no evil star.

Rats paraded a rapstar.

Raw Novel? Lev on War.

Red I.V.? I derail Ali, a redivider.

Red root put up to order.

Red rum, sir, is murder.

*Half Empty
or Half Full ?

Chemistry Has The Answer!

Air is a gas mixture that contains by volume, 78.09% nitrogen, 20.95% oxygen, 0.93% argon, 0.039% carbon dioxide, and small amounts of other gases. Air also contains a variable amount of water vapor, on average around 1% at sea level.

H2O. Water molecules. Oxygen bound to two hydrogen atoms.

*The Glass Is Full !

Repel a leper.

Retracting, I sign it, Carter.

Revered now, I live on. O did I do no evil, I wonder, ever?

"Reviled did I live," said I, "as evil I did deliver!"

Reward drawer.

Rise to vote sir.

Ron! OH! Sex in a Toyota nixes honor!

Rot a renegade, wed a generator.

"Rum... rum..." I murmur.

Salt an atlas.

Satan, oscillate my metallic sonatas!

Saw tide rose? So red it was.

See, slave, I demonstrate yet arts no medieval sees.

HELP ME . . .

I Had Fun Once!

It Was Awful!

Can you help me find a better, more mundane life? Can you rescue me from levity and frivolity?
I need someone to love me, quietly!
Call 259-555-1212

Sega? Millions! Alas, no ill images!

Selim's tired – no wonder, it's miles!

Semite times.

Senile felines.

Seven eves.

Sex at noon taxes.

Sex-aware era waxes.

Sh…Tom sees moths.

Sir, I eye Iris.

Sir, I'm Iris.

"Sissy as a nana" says sis.

Sit on a potato pan Otis!

Slap a ham on Omaha, pals.

Smart rams.

MISSING

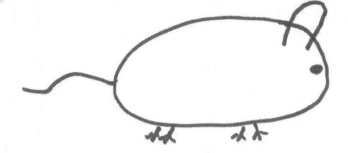

He answers to the name Maximus Decimus Meridius, Commander of the Armies of the North, General of the Felix Legions, Loyal Servant to the True Emperor Marcus Aurelius. Father to a murdered son, husband to a murdered wife. And, he will have his vengeance, in this life or the next.

Generally friendly unless cornered or threatened.

If Found, please return to the Colosseum, Piazza del Colosseo, 1 00184, Rome, Italy
or
Call 011 + 39 + 06-1212

So Ida, adios.

So many dynamos!

So, cat tacos!

Solo gigolos.

Some emos

Some men interpret nine memos.

Soreya, say eros.

Stab nail at ill Italian bats.

Stack cats.

Star comedy by Democrats.

Star rats.

Star? Come, Donna Melba, I'm an amiable man –
no Democrats!

Stella won no wallets.

Step on no pets.

**The Chemical Composition
of Some People Around Here
Makes Them . . .**

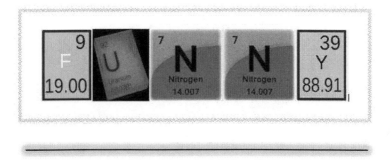

Step pals never even slap pets.

Steven, I left an oily lion at feline vets.

Stop on no pots.

Stop pots.

Stop! Murder us not, tonsured rumpots!

Strap on no parts.

Straw warts.

Straw? No, too stupid a fad; I put soot on warts.

Stressed desserts.

Stressed was I ere I saw desserts.

Stressed? No tips? Spit on desserts.

Stunt nuts.

Sums are not set as a test on Erasmus.

Swap God for a janitor; rot in a jar of dog paws.

PERSPECTIVE

Physicist: 0 & 650 nm + 510 nm + 475 nm

Radiologist:

Computer Engineer: 0000 & 1111

Cardiologist: ——————— &

Electrician: 0 & 120

Pianist:

Web Master: #000000 & #FFFFFF

Signer: &

T. Eliot, top bard, notes putrid tang emanating, is sad. I'd assign it a name: gnat dirt upset on drab pot-toilet.

Tahitti hat.

Tangy gnat.

Tarzan raised Desi Arnaz' rat.

Tell a ballet.

Ten animals I slam in a net.

Test tube butt set.

Tide net safe soon; a noose fastened it.

"Tie Mandie," I'd name it.

Tino dump mud on it.

Tips spill, lips spit.

Tis but a tub. Sit.

To idiot.

GAUDY STOUT WALKS INTO A BAR. THE BARTENDER SAYS,

"We don't serve your type here!"

Todd erases a red dot.

Tons I tore his kayaks – I, hero, 'tis not.

Tons o' snot.

Too bad I hid a boot.

Too far, Edna, we wander afoot.

Too hot to hoot.

Top spot.

Top step's pup's pet spot.

Trays simple help, missy art!

Tsetse's test.

Tube debut.

Tulsa night life: filth, gin, a slut.

Tuna nut.

Tuna roll or a nut?

If
Lorenzo Romano
Amedeo Carlo Avogadro
C a l l s . . .

Ask him to leave his number!

UFO tofu.

Walmart's tram law.

Wanna tan? Naw.

Warsaw was raw.

Was it a bar or a bat I saw?

Was it a bat I saw?

Was it a car or a cat I saw?

Was it a cat I saw?

Was it a rat I saw?

Was it Eliot's toilet I saw?

Waste Pa, pet saw.

We few.

We panic in a pew.

We sew, ewe sew.

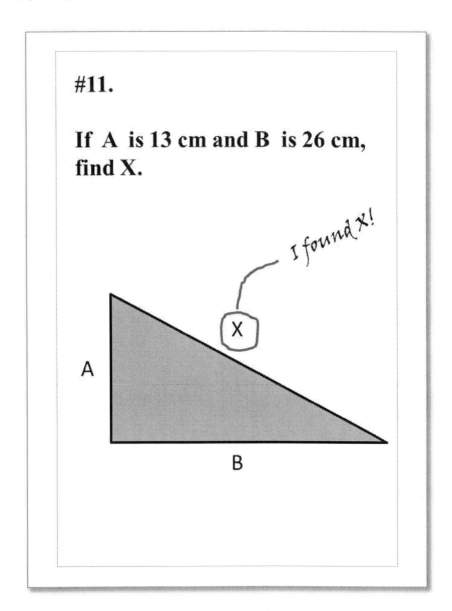

We sew.

Wet sanitary rat in a stew.

Wet stew.

Wo Nemo toss a lasso to me now!

Won kiosk. So, I know.

Won tons? Not now.

Won't I panic in a pit now?

Won't it now?

Won't lovers revolt now?

Wonder if Sununu's fired now.

Wonders in Italy, Latin is red now.

Wonton? Not now.

Ya, Decaf. FACE DAY!!

Ya! Pizza zip pizazz! I pay.

MISSING

My Pet Turtle, - answers to the
name Tao Fu. He took my
Nun-chucks, & Throwing Stars

Tao Fu seems slow but he is very dangerous.
Don't corner him – just call me, 011 + 86 +
0555-1212. Eventually he will come home –
he has disappeared before.   In the mean time,
evil-doer's beware!

Yawn a more Roman way.

Yawn...Madonna fan? No damn way!

Ye boil! I obey!

Yen o' money.

Yo banana boy!

Yo bozo boy!

Yo bro! Free beer for boy!

Yo, banana boy!

Yo, Bob! Mug o' gumbo, boy!

Yo, bottoms up! U.S. motto, boy.

Yreka Bakery.

Zeus was deified, saw Suez.

PARAPRODOKIANS

My friend Bill, also explained Paraprodokians to me:

"A **paraprosdokian** is a sentence or phrase that presents a twist which is surprising or unexpected in a way that causes you to re-interpret the first part."

Bill Schmidt, 1967

Wikipedia further explains:

"Paraprosdokian" comes from the Greek "against" and "expectation". The term "prosdokia" ("expectation") occurs with the preposition "para" in Greek rhetorical writers of the 1st century BCE and the 1st and 2nd centuries CE, with the meaning "contrary to expectation" or "unexpectedly". Canadian linguist and etymology author William Gordon Casselman argues that, while the word is now in wide circulation, "paraprosdokian" (or "paraprodokia") is not a term of classical (or medieval) Greek or Latin rhetoric, but a late 20th-century neologism. The word does not yet appear in the Oxford English Dictionary.

Other sources attribute the term directly to the German philosopher Gustav Gerber. There is record of the ancient Greeks using such figures of speech for both comedy and philosophy. Indeed, many modern comics and notable individuals have made good use of the paraprosdokian.

Hope you enjoy this collection.

A CASE FOR DRINKING

Because no good story ever got started by someone eating a salad!

I asked God for a bike, but I know God doesn't work that way. So I stole a bike and asked for forgiveness.

Do not argue with an idiot. He will drag you down to his level and beat you with experience.

I want to die peacefully in my sleep, like my grandfather. Not screaming and yelling like the passengers in his car.

Going to church doesn't make you a Christian any more than standing in a garage makes you a car.

The last thing I want to do is hurt you. But it's still on the list.

Light travels faster than sound. This is why some people appear bright until you hear them speak.

If I agreed with you, we'd both be wrong.

We never really grow up; we only learn how to act in public.

War does not determine who is right – only who is left.

Peace is that quiet when everyone is reloading.

Knowledge is knowing a tomato is a fruit; Wisdom is not putting it in a fruit salad.

Evening news is where they begin with 'Good evening' and then proceed to tell you why it isn't.

To steal ideas from one person is plagiarism. To steal from many is research.

A bus station is where a bus stops. A train station is where a train stops. On my desk, I have a work station.

How is it one careless match can start a forest fire, but it takes a whole box to start a campfire?

Some people are like Slinkies: not really good for anything, but you can't help smiling when you see one tumble down the stairs.

NOTICE

I'm relatively sure that I have successfully invented a time machine. If my experiment goes well, I'll materialize at exactly 11:40 AM this Saturday morning.

As a courtesy, I am giving you plenty of notice so you aren't standing at this spot when I return – otherwise the situation could get ugly.

Left for **06-06-1966**, last Saturday morning.

BTW – I won't be returning in some weird machine, a red British Phone Booth, or in A DeLorean. I also won't be naked, half fly – half human, or appear with three eyes. If that's want you're thinking you've watched way too many F'ing Sci-Fi movies!

If I don't materialize check back at 11:40 AM next Sunday. If not then, check my garage at 304 Hickman St. If not there, I'll see you on the other side! John.

Dolphins are so smart that within a few weeks of captivity, they can train people to stand on the very edge of the pool and throw them fish.

I didn't say it was your fault; I said I was blaming you.

Why does someone believe you when you say there are four billion stars but check when you say the paint is wet?

Why do Americans choose from just two people to run for president and 50 for Miss America ?

Behind every successful man is his woman. Behind the fall of a successful man is usually another woman.

A clear conscience is usually the sign of a bad memory.

You do not need a parachute to skydive. You only need a parachute to skydive twice.

NOTICE GIVEN!

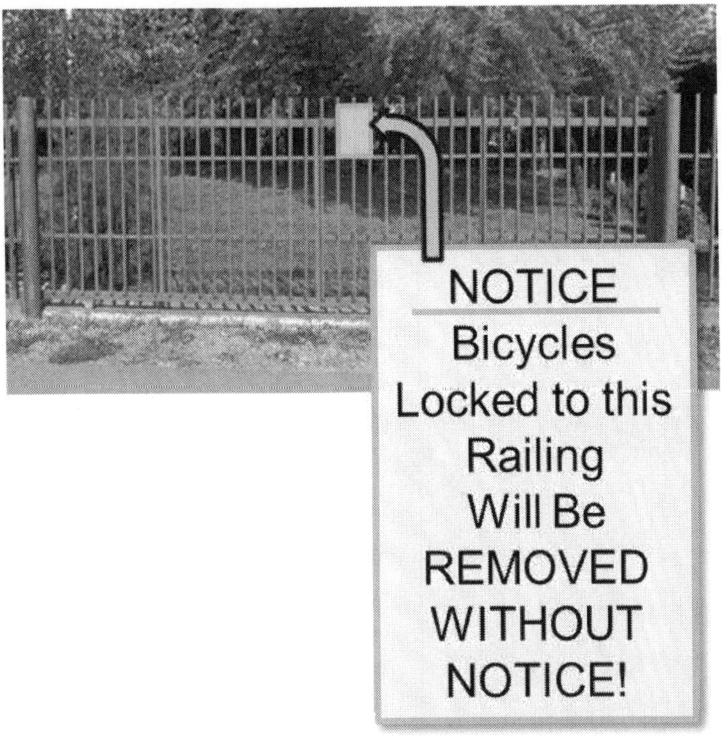

The voices in my head may not be real, but they have some good ideas!

Always borrow money from a pessimist. He won't expect it back.

A diplomat is someone who can tell you to go to hell in such a way that you will look forward to the trip.

Hospitality: making your guests feel like they're at home, even if you wish they were.

Money can't buy happiness, but it sure makes misery easier to live with.

Some cause happiness wherever they go. Others whenever they go.

I used to be indecisive. Now I'm not sure.

When tempted to fight fire with fire, remember that the Fire Department usually uses water.

HELP WANTED

Seeking flunkies and minions.
Evil Genius has immediate openings.

Requirements:

- Must work 24/7
- Enjoy working with fascist psychopath
- Costumes and death ray guns provided
- Hi-tech communicators provided
- Accept miserably low pay
- Potentially sacrifice life to help obtain world dominion
- Miserable & painful death probable
- No <u>Weirdos</u>!

- Call for Interview: **666-666-MWAH**

You're never too old to learn something stupid.

To be sure of hitting the target, shoot first and call whatever you hit the target.

Nostalgia isn't what it used to be.

Some people hear voices. Some see invisible people. Others have no imagination whatsoever.

A bus is a vehicle that runs twice as fast when you are after it as when you are in it.

If you are supposed to learn from your mistakes, why do some people have more than one child?

Change is inevitable, except from a vending machine.

The car stopped on a dime, which unfortunately was in a pedestrian's pocket.

Where there's a will, I want to be in it.

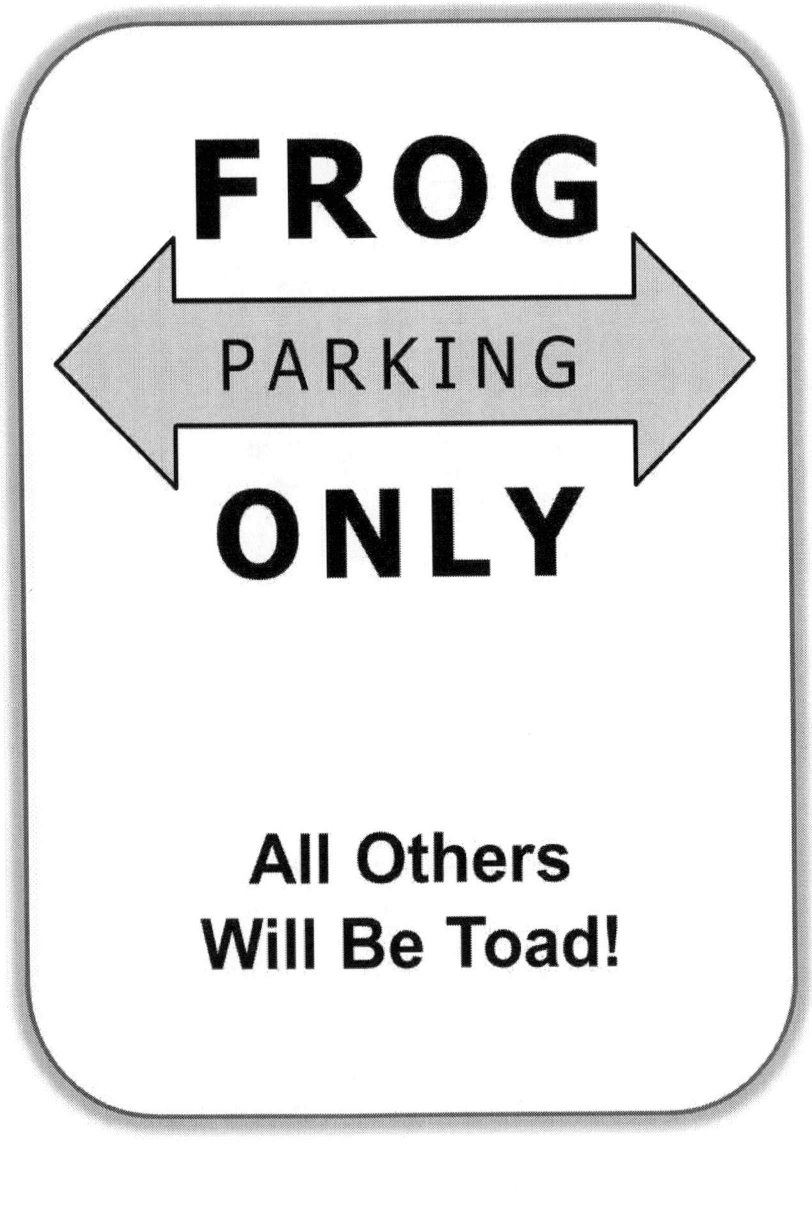
FROG
PARKING
ONLY
All Others
Will Be Toad!

Before you criticize a man, walk a mile in his shoes. That way, you will be a mile away and he won't have any shoes.

Two guys walked into a bar. The third one ducked.

The early bird might get the worm, but the second mouse gets the cheese.

I thought I wanted a career; turns out I just wanted pay checks.

A bank is a place that will lend you money, if you can prove that you don't need it.

Whenever I fill out an application, in the part that says in an emergency, notify, I put A DOCTOR.

I discovered I scream the same way whether I'm about to be devoured by a great white shark or if a piece of seaweed touches my foot.

School: Spelling Rule . . .

I Before E,

**Except
After C**

WEIRD !

If you're not part of the solution, you're part of the precipitate. — Henry J. Tillman

The saying 'Getting there is half the fun' became obsolete with the advent of commercial airlines. — Henry J. Tillman

A fool and his money are soon elected. — Will Rogers

Ohio claims they are due a president as they haven't had one since Taft. Look at the United States, they have not had one since Lincoln.
— Will Rogers

If I am reading this graph correctly, I would be very surprised. — Stephen Colbert

There's a bunch of different crunches that affect the abs ... my favorite is Nestle. — Shmuel Breban

When I was 10, I beat up the school bully. His arms were in casts. That's what gave me the courage.
— Emo Philips

QUIDQUID LATINE DICTUM SIT,

Graeca ad me sonat!

(Whatever it is, it sounds Greek to me!)

I can picture in my mind a world without war, a world without hate. And I can picture us attacking that world, because they'd never expect it.
— Jack Handey

It has been said that democracy is the worst form of government except all those other forms that have been tried. — Winston Churchill

You can always count on Americans to do the right thing — after they've tried everything else.
— Winston Churchill

Time flies like an arrow; fruit flies like a banana.
— Groucho Marx

She got her good looks from her father; he's a plastic surgeon. — Groucho Marx

One morning I shot an elephant in my pajamas. How he got in my pajamas I'll never know.
— Groucho Marx

Outside of a dog, a book is man's best friend. Inside of a dog, it's too dark to read.
— Groucho Marx

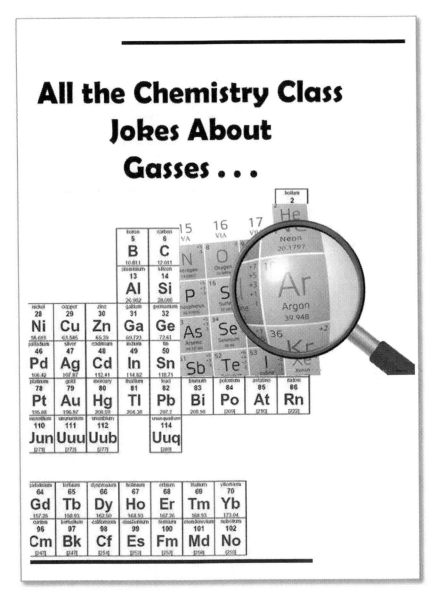

All the Chemistry Class
Jokes About
Gasses . . .

I've had a perfectly wonderful evening, but this wasn't it. — Groucho Marx

If you can't sleep, count sheep. Don't count endangered animals. You will run out.

A fly was very close to being called a land, because that's what it does half the time.

I want to rob a bank with a BB gun. Give me all your money or I will give you a dimple! I will be rich, you will be cute. We both win.

I had a chicken finger that was so big, it was a chicken hand.

I got binoculars 'cause I don't want to go that close.

I can read minds, but I'm illiterate.

If Spiderman was real, and I was a criminal, and he shot me with his web, I would say, Dude, thanks for the hammock.

I got a belt on that's holding up my pants, and the pants have belt loops that hold up the belt. What's going on here? Who is the real hero?

I had the cab driver drive me here backwards, and the dude owed me $27.50.

Kittens play with yarn, they bat it around. What they're really doing is saying, I can't knit, get this away from me!

I met this girl, she was an actress, and she gave me her number. It started with 555.

If you don't know a light bulb is a three-way light bulb, it messes with your head. You reach to turn it off, and it just gets brighter! That's the exact opposite of what I wanted you to do! So you turn the switch again, and it gets brighter once more! I will break you, light bulb!

I went to a restaurant with my friend, and he said, "Pass the salt." I said, Screw you! Sit closer to the salt.

Imagine if the headless horseman had a headless horse. That would be chaos. I would think that if you were the headless horseman's horse, you would be thinking, "I don't think this dude can see".

I belong to no organized party. I am a Democrat.
— Will Rogers

If you are going through hell, keep going.
— Winston Churchill

I haven't slept for ten days, because that would be too long. — Mitch Hedberg

Take my wife — please. — Henny Youngman

ENGINEER CHEER

E to the X, Dy, Dx,

E to the X, Dx.

Cosine, Secant,

Tangent, Sine,

3.14159,

Square Root, Cube Root, BTU,

Slip Stick, Slide Rule,

Hail Purdue!

There's a fine line between cuddling and holding someone down so they can't get away.

I always take life with a grain of salt ... plus a slice of lemon ... and a shot of tequila.

I used to be conceited, but now I'm perfect.

When chemists die, they barium.

Jokes about German sausage are the wurst.

I know a guy who's addicted to brake fluid. He says he can stop any time.

How does Moses make his tea? Hebrews it.

I stayed up all night to see where the sun went. Then it dawned on me.

When you hear this Pick-up Line . . .
How 'bout I buy you a drink?
I've got a Ferrari. Wanna go for a spin?
Wanna go for a fried egg sandwich?

Just say loudly . . .

HOW ABOUT OH HELL TO THE NO!

This girl said she recognized me from the vegetarian club, but I'd never met herbivore.

I'm reading a book about anti-gravity. I just can't put it down.

I did a theatrical performance about puns. It was a play on words.

They told me I had type-A blood, but it was a Type-O.

PMS jokes aren't funny; period.

Why were the Indians here first? They had reservations.

We are going on a class trip to the Coca-Cola factory. I hope there's no pop quiz.

I didn't like my beard at first. Then it grew on me.

Did you hear about the cross-eyed teacher who lost her job because she couldn't control her pupils?

When you get a bladder infection urine trouble.

Broken pencils are pointless.

I tried to catch some fog, but I mist.

What do you call a dinosaur with an extensive vocabulary? A thesaurus.

England has no kidney bank, but it does have a Liverpool.

I used to be a banker, but then I lost interest.

I dropped out of communism class because of lousy Marx.

All the toilets in New York's police stations have been stolen. The police have nothing to go on.

MOVING SALE

Moving to Nepal as Foreign Correspondent. Can't take library – must liquidate. Taking favorite Chinese cook book isn't politically correct. Rare – only 100 or so printed in US. Will Sacrifice! $20 OBO

663-555-1212
663-555-1212
663-555-1212
663-555-1212
663-555-1212
663-555-1212
663-555-1212
663-555-1212

I got a job at a bakery because I kneaded dough.

Haunted French pancakes give me the crepes.

Velcro, what a rip off!

A cartoonist was found dead in his home. Details are sketchy.

Venison for dinner again? Oh deer!

The earthquake in Washington obviously was the government's fault.

Be kind to your dentist, he has fillings too.

I was visiting with my kids last night when I asked if I could borrow a newspaper. This is the 21st century, they said. We don't waste money on newspapers. Here, you can use my iPad. I can tell you this: That roach never knew what hit it.

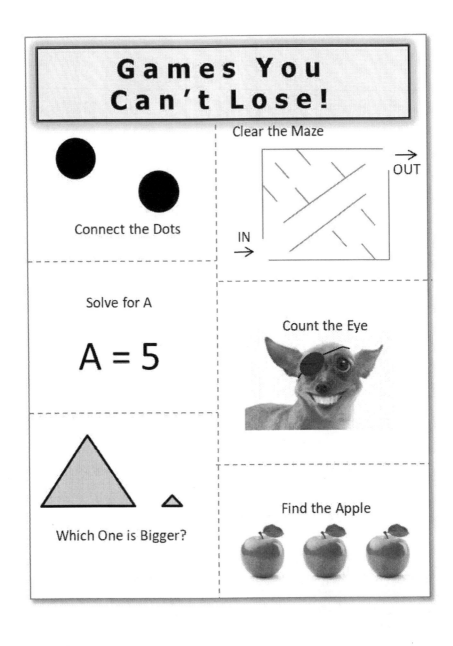

Games You Can't Lose!

Connect the Dots

Clear the Maze

IN →

OUT →

Solve for A

A = 5

Count the Eye

Which One is Bigger?

Find the Apple

One thing that humbles me deeply is to see that human genius has its limits while human stupidity does not.

Silence is golden, duct tape is silver.

Any man who can drive safely while kissing a pretty girl is simply not giving the kiss the attention it deserves.

I tried to drown my sorrows, but the bastards learned how to swim.

Atheism is always not for prophet.

She looks as though she's been poured into her clothes, and forgot to say 'when'.

Go to heaven for the climate, Hell for the company.

I wondered why the baseball was getting bigger. Then it hit me.

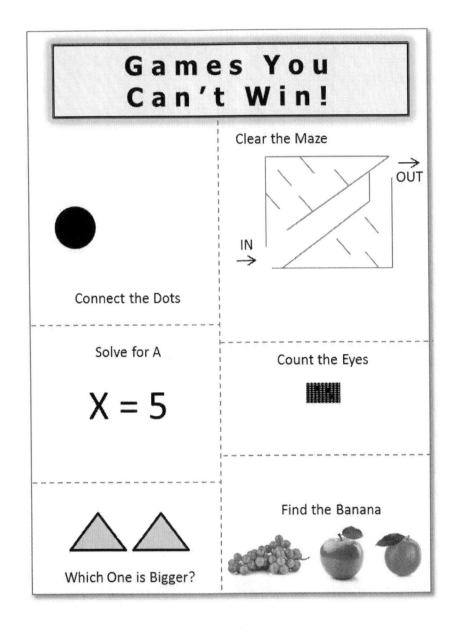

Give a lawyer a fire, he'll be warm for a day. Set a lawyer on fire, he'll be warm for the rest of his life.

I saw a woman wearing a sweat shirt with Guess on it . . . so I said Implants?

I admit I have a tremendous sex drive. My boyfriend lives forty miles away.

All I ask is the chance to prove that money can't make me happy.

It was impossible to get a conversation going, everybody was talking too much.

There are 10 kinds of people in the world: Those that understand binary and those that don't.

Always swim or dive with a friend. It reduces your chance of shark attack by 50%.

Eat what you want and if someone lectures you about it, eat them too!

Well, I'm having a great day. Woke up this morning, got out of bed, went to the bathroom. In that order!

I don't know why they told me I'm innumerate, it doesn't add up.

Of course men can multitask, we read in the bathroom.

Growing old is tough not growing old is worse.

A fine is a tax on doing bad, so a tax must be a fine for doing good.

The fly was very close to being called the land, because that's what it does half the time.

I'm missing you and my aim is improving.

I like going to the park and watching the children run and jump around, because you see, they don't know I'm using blanks.

I LIVE IN CONSTANT FEAR
THAT THE NEW ADMINSTRATION
WILL DEPORT MY LATINA
MOTHER-IN-LAW,
ISABELLA FLOREZ.

SHE LIVES AT
706 HICKMAN ROAD,
COLLIER, IL.
(IN THE BLUE HOUSE)

SHE GETS HOME FROM WORK
AT 6 PM

If all the girls at Vassar were laid end to end, I wouldn't be surprised.

As a child my family's menu consisted of two choices: take it or leave it.

Any time three New Yorkers get into a cab without an argument, a bank has just been robbed.
— Phyllis Diller

I always thought it was polite to open the door for a lady but she just screamed and flew out of the plane.

I try to watch what I eat and yet my eyes just aren't quick enough.

Two wrongs don't make a right, three lefts do.

Women's rights impress me as much as their lefts.

The practice of mindfulness may show you what's so. Further enlightenment will show you, so what.

KNOW THESE PEOPLE?

1. Monica Lewinski
2. Bill Clinton
3. Barrack Obama
4. Donald Trump
5. Jorge Bergoglio
6. Anthony Weiner
7. Vladimir Putin
8. Linda Lovelace
9. Saddam Hussein
10. Tiger Woods
11. George Bush

Know them all but #5?
So – You know all of the Liars, Criminals, Adulterers, Murderers, Sluts, and Cheaters, but you don't know the Pope?

Humanity has achieved, abiding love, peace, progress, truth, beauty, glory, enlightenment and tolerance, on paper.

If you're telekinetic raise my hand.

Pet spiders are cheaper to buy off the web.

A broken pencil is pointless.

We don't stop playing because we grow old - we grow old because we stop playing.

Newton stayed up all night puzzling the movement of the sun then it dawned on him.

You are what you eat, may contains nuts.

I hate to say I told you so, so I am going to shout it really loud.

A bad banker quickly loses interest.

9 Points to Ponder

- Death is the number 1 killer in the world.

- Life is sexually transmitted.

- Good health is merely the slowest possible rate at which one can die.

- Men have two emotions: hungry and horny, and they can't tell them apart. If you see a gleam in his eyes, make him a sandwich.

- Give a person a fish and you feed them for a day. Teach a person to use the Internet and s/he won't bother you for weeks, months, maybe years.

- Health nuts are going to feel stupid someday, lying in the hospital, dying of nothing.

- All of us could take a lesson from the weather. It pays no attention to criticism.

- In the 60s, people took acid to make the world weird. Now the world is weird, and people take Prozac to make it normal.

- Life is like a jar of jalapeno peppers. What you do today might burn your butt tomorrow.

- **Don't worry about old age; it doesn't last that long.**

The faults of the burglar are the qualities of the financier.

Age is an issue of mind over matter. If you don't mind, it doesn't matter.

Be careful about reading health books. You may die of a misprint.

Strong emotions are stupid and should be hated!

Work is the curse of the drinking class.

Your argument is sound, just sound, lots of sound.

I'm not being rude. You're just insignificant.

I don't know what your problem is, but I'll bet it's hard to pronounce.

If you see a bomb technician running, try to keep up with him.

You
Have
To
Be
Odd
To
Be
Number
One

One thing you mustn't miss when you visit Cleveland is the plane.

I don't approve of political jokes. I've seen too many of them get elected.

To keep fit my grandmother walks five miles a day. She's 97 now and we have no idea where she is.

Laughter is the best medicine, if you don't have insurance.

I miss my ex so often, I really need a laser sight.

Clothes maketh the man. Naked people have little or no influence at all.

Nothing is possible, I've been doing it for years.

Celery is 95% water and 100% not pizza.

I'd tell you an Ebola joke, but you won't get it.

Don't Read The Rest Of This Message!

You Just HAD to do it, Didn't You!
Aren't You a Little Malcontent!

For every complex problem, there is an answer that is short, simple and wrong. — H.L. Mencken

Women will never be equal to men until they can walk down the street with a bald head and a beer gut, and still think they are sexy.

That dress fits you perfectly... if you were dead for two weeks.

As a kid I was the youngest and always getting beat up by the two oldest. Mom and Dad!

No matter how much money you give a homeless man for some coffee, you never get that coffee, do you?

I stayed up all night playing poker with tarot cards. I got a full house and four people died.

I used to work in a fire hydrant factory. You couldn't park anywhere near the place.

UNDERSTANDING "F·ON·IK·S"

If the "GH" sound in Enou<u>gh</u>
is pronounced "F",

and the "O" in Women
makes the short "I" sound,

and the TI in Na<u>ti</u>on
is pronounced "SH",

Then the word
"GHOTI"

Is pronounced
"FISH"

I went to a restaurant that serves breakfast at any time. So I ordered French toast during the Renaissance.

Eagles may soar but weasels don't get sucked into jet engines.

If god didn't want us to eat cows, he wouldn't make them out of beef.

Recent research confirms sex during pregnancy is safe, except when caught cheating.

If green leafy vegetables are good for us why do they taste like shit?

A man enters a sushi restaurant. The chef asks him how he'd like his sushi and the man says, well done.

My parents tried to surprise me with a car when I was 16 but they missed.

I'm supposed to respect my elders, but it's getting harder and harder for me to find one now.

FOR SALE
Spinning Wheel

Almost brand new. Works Great! For Homebody with an antique, quaint, esoteric hobby or a for a post-apocalyptic, kick-ass, gonna-survive, gonna rebuild humanity, starting–over, survivalist.

Price:
1 Oz 24k Gold

221-555-1212　221-555-1212　221-555-1212　221-555-1212　221-555-1212　221-555-1212　221-555-1212　221-555-1212　221-555-1212　221-555-1212　221-555-1212　221-555-1212

I don't care to belong to a club that accepts people like me as members.

I find television very educating. Every time somebody turns on the set, I go into the other room and read a book.

Where there's a will, there are relatives.

There but for the grace of God—goes God.

When I was young, I thought that money was the most important thing in life. Now that I'm old, I know it is. —Oscar Wilde

My boyfriend and I broke up, even though we're still deeply in love. He wanted to get married, and I didn't want him to. — Rita Rudner

Last night in bed, we lost power, and the electricity went out too.

Some people ask me why I walk in my sleep. I tell them it's safer than running.

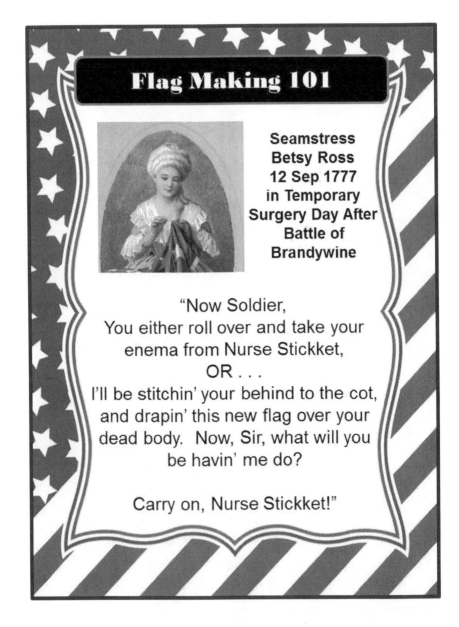

Seeing the light at the end of the tunnel can be disturbing, if you took the bridge.

I know a guy who picked up a 300-pound hitchhiker. He has the hernia to prove it.

Everyone seems to want athletic arms and athletic legs, but nobody wants athlete's foot.

An enigma is a mystery without a solution, but an enema is a mysterious solution.

I love cooking, as long as someone else does it.

Children should be seen and not herded.

It takes 8,460 bolts to assemble an automobile, and one nut to scatter it all over the road.

There is usually only a limited amount of damage that can be done by dull or stupid people. For creating a truly monumental disaster, you need people with high IQs. — Thomas Sowell

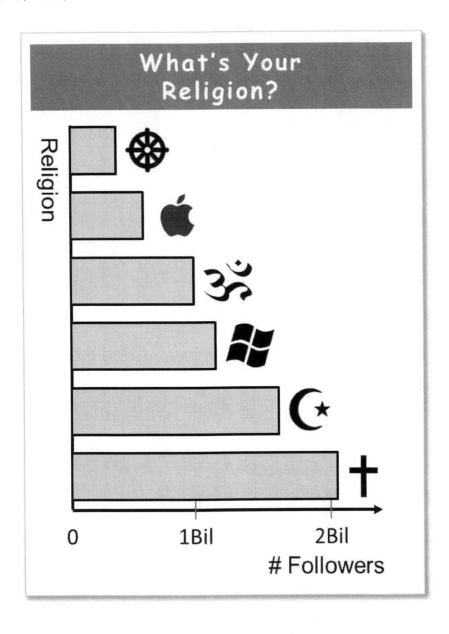

Everybody is a genius. But if you judge a fish by its ability to climb a tree, it will live its whole life believing that it is stupid. — Albert Einstein

When one person suffers from a delusion it is called insanity; when many people suffer from a delusion it is called religion. — Robert Pirsig

Religion has convinced people that there's an invisible man living in the sky, who watches everything you do every minute of every day. And the invisible man has a list of ten specific things he doesn't want you to do. And if you do any of these things, he will send you to a special place, of burning and fire and smoke and torture and anguish for you to live forever, and suffer and burn and scream until the end of time. But he loves you. He loves you and he needs money. — George Carlin

All religions are the same: religion is basically guilt, with different holidays.— Cathy Ladman

A consensus means that everyone agrees to say collectively what no one believes individually.
— Abba Eban

ABOUT KARMA

An ingenious appraisal system.

Has no menu. You get served what you deserve!

I Saw that!

Don't Take Revenge. Karma get's those who hurt you. If lucky, God will let you watch!

It's pronounced, "Ha Ha, F-you!"

List of People You Missed: Sophia, Lindsey, Olive, & Emma

Men do make passes at girls who wear glasses; it depends on their frames. — Dorothy Parker

A successful man is one who makes more money than his wife can spend. A successful woman is one who can find such a man. — Lana Turner

Marriage is like a public toilet. Those waiting outside are desperate to get in and those inside are desperate to come out.

Experience is something you don't get until just after you need it.

Success is the ability to go from one failure to another with no loss of enthusiasm.
— Winston Churchill

The height of embarrassment is when two sets of eyes meet through a keyhole.

We took some pictures of the native girls, but they're not developed yet. We're going back next year, when they're more developed.
— Groucho Marx

Fran's Tips

HIKING TODAY?

DON'T FORGET YOUR COMPASS!

IT'S AWKWARD WHEN YOU HAVE TO EAT YOUR FRIENDS!

A boiled egg is hard to beat.

You can tune a piano... but you can't tuna fish.

The police at a daycare center had to deal with a child who was resisting a rest.

When you've seen one shopping center, you've seen a mall.

When she saw her first strand of grey hair, she wanted to dye.

A worker fell into an upholstery machine and now he's fully recovered.

He had a photographic memory, but he never developed it.

A young man had his entire left side cut-off. He's all right now.

When a clock is hungry, it goes back four seconds.

GO WITH THE FLO . . .

Florence
Nightingale
1854

Florence
Sabin
1901

Florence
Harding
1921

Florence
Price
1933

Florence
Joyner
1984

Progressive
Flo
2008

A bicycle can't stand alone. It's just too tired.

Why do we drive on a parkway and park in a driveway?

He was a skilled archer, though he did occasionally miss his wife.

I read an article on the serious dangers of drinking too much alcohol and it scared the crap out of me! From now on, no more reading!

The reformed gambler was told twelve-step meetings help, but don't bet on it.

When fish are in schools, they sometimes take debate.

A thief who stole a calendar got twelve months.

When the smog lifts in Los Angeles U.C.L.A.

The batteries were given free of charge.

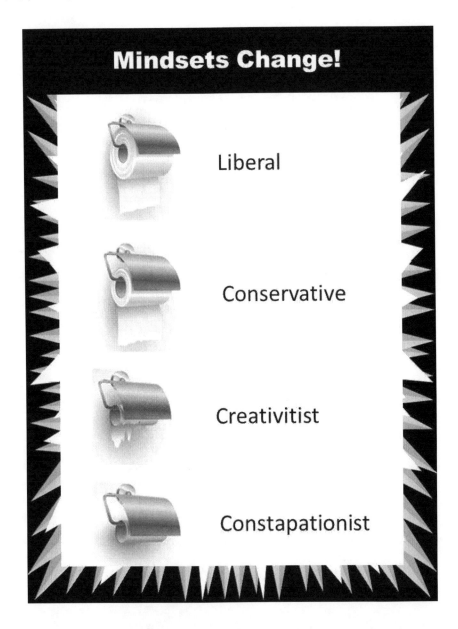

A dentist and a manicurist married. They fought tooth and nail.

A will is a dead giveaway.

Acupuncture is a jab well done. That's the point of it.

Those who get too big for their pants will be exposed in the end.

I've been in love with the same woman for forty-one years. If my wife finds out, she'll kill me.
— Henny Youngman

My wife and I were happy for twenty years. Then we met. — Rodney Dangerfield

I installed a skylight in my apartment; the people who live above me are furious — Steven Wright

Think Outside The Box!

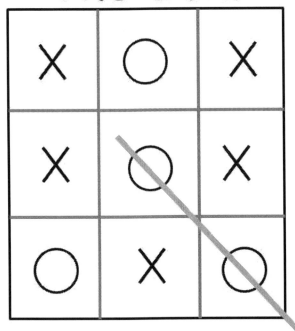

Never Another
Cat's Game!

Ants are always healthy because they have little antibodies

Is there ever a day that mattresses aren't on sale?

What happens if you get scared half-to-death twice?

Whet to the Air and Space Museum, but nothing was there!

All those who believe in psychokinesis, raise my hand.

Hold the door for a clown! It's a nice jester.

If pride comes before a fall, then humility should come by winter.

Ban pre-shredded cheese. Make America grate again!

I just did a week's worth of cardio after walking into a spider web!

AUTHOR

RAND GEE

Rand is a 35 year-old story-teller and humorist trapped in 65 year-old body. He is always on the lookout for another real-life character, joke, a strange bulletin board posting, a bit of visual irony, or another well-crafted palindrome or paraprosdokian for his collection.

Be cautious about engaging with him in conversation. The way he spins stories, you won't know if he is telling the truth or a bold-faced lie, until he smiles.

To schedule Rand for a speaking engagement, e-mail him at randgee@charter.net

GRAPHIC ARTIST

KEN KUZIA

Ken produced the cover image.

Born in the 40's, but a child of the 60's, Ken Kuzia has reshaped his perspective on art as frequently as he has changed his media.   He has progressed through stages of drawing, painting, sculpture, woodworking, and has arrived at digital photography and videography. Who knows what's next!

Ken's art is personal to him, as with most artists who try to convey what they consider to be interesting or provoking. However, evoking some feeling or reaction from the viewer is also a goal.

Aside from the visual arts, Ken flirts with writing based upon his experiences growing up in the southern tier of New York State and

141

migrating to the Finger Lakes region. Ken is also a charter member and president of the Victor Art Group in Victor, New York.

Feel free to stop by Ken's web site to view other portraits and scenes. The site is located at:

http://vicartgroup.wixsite.com/the-art-of-ken-kuzia

Ken Kuzia

Cover Photo & Design

Editing

Deposit Photo & Fotolia

Licensed Photos throughout from DepositPhoto.com and Fotolia.com.

Made in the USA
Monee, IL
09 May 2020